MOOSE

MOOSE

JACK DENTON SCOTT

photographs by
OZZIE SWEET

G. P. PUTNAM'S SONS
New York

Text copyright © 1981 by Jack Denton Scott.
Photographs copyright © 1981 by Ozzie Sweet.
All rights reserved. Published simultaneously in
Canada by Academic Press Canada Limited, Toronto.
Printed in the United States of America.
First impression.
Library of Congress Cataloging in Publication Data
Scott, Jack Denton.
Moose.
Summary: Presents the moose, that northern
creature which is the "world's largest living deer."
1. Moose—Juvenile literature.   [1. Moose]
I. Sweet, Ozzie.   II. Title.
QL737.U55S37   599.73'57   81-5152AACR2
ISBN 0-399-20721-X
Book design by Kathleen Westray

For my wife
Diane,
without whose interest and help
many of the moose photographs
would not have been possible.
O.S.

MOOSE country is wild country.

If one is fortunate enough to see a moose standing outlined against a rugged mountain background or browsing contentedly on a grassy hillside, then the setting must be isolated wilderness. For while the moose shares its range with many wild creatures, humans are not among them.

Today moose can be found throughout Alaska, down through the deep dark forests of Canada, in Maine in the East, and on the forest lands of the Grand Tetons in Wyoming in the West. And moose are found in other states as well. They inhabit parts of New Hampshire and Vermont, Montana, Idaho, Colorado, Minnesota and Michigan. Isle Royale National Park in Michigan is a favorite place for naturalists to observe moose living in balance with a large predator, the wolf. Because Isle Royale is an island in Lake Superior with no access to the mainland for either animal, it provides a naturally controlled setting in which to observe both species.

In wilderness areas, moose live alongside many harmless creatures, among them small ground squirrels, snowy Dall sheep that live on the slopes and peaks of mountain ranges, and stately caribou in the far north. But other large and

potentially dangerous residents are not so harmless. The giant grizzly, the largest and fiercest of the bears, is the most serious threat to the moose. When grizzlies are around, young moose and old nervously scent the wind and instantly seek the nearest natural cover.

The gigantic moose, which seems to dominate its territory by sheer size and strength alone, has learned to take advantage of its total environment. Be it lake, pond, grassy plain or spruce forest, moose can usually find sustenance on the land or in the water.

One of the more dramatic sights nature has to offer is this huge, awkward-looking animal, standing on the shore of a lake looking out at its vastness, then suddenly plunging into its freezing shallows and skillfully swimming out into the deep until it seems to vanish.

Although moose are masters of their environment and majestic in size, a close-up look at a physically perfect cow or bull resembles a genetically mixed-up mule with its long, doleful face and droopy muzzle.

Looking as though it has been assembled by nature in an ironic mood, the moose seems to be made up of the spare parts of other animals. It has an almost comic 3- or 4-inch tail on a body that averages 8 to 10 feet from tail to nose, distinctly humped shoulders, flaring mane and an ostentatious "goatee," a useless flap of skin covered with long hair called a dewlap, or "bell," that hangs down from its throat. And if it is a bull moose, all this is topped off by an unbelievable set of antlers. One naturalist said, "Seeing a full-grown moose for the first time, you don't know whether to laugh or cry."

The moose stands higher than a horse on its 4-foot stiltlike legs, some moose measuring as high as 7 feet at the shoulder. Adult cows weigh as much as 800 pounds and bulls weigh between 900 and 1,400 pounds. In Alaska, bulls weighing as much as 1,800 pounds have been found.

What are these unusual creatures and where do they come from?

It is likely that moose crossed a continent-linking, glacier-formed strip of land at Alaska's Bering Strait, approximately 175,000 years ago during the Pleistocene period. Walking out of the Ice Age, they roamed across the frozen waste into what is today Canada and our northern states, south along the Atlantic coast as far as the Carolinas. Still prehistoric in appearance, the moose has changed not at all from that long ago harsh era.

Actually this great mammal evolved from a cat-sized creature that first appeared on earth more than 45 million years ago during the Oligocene period; it took another 10 million years to grow antlers and 35 million years more to evolve to its present size.

Belonging to the family Cervidae, which includes caribou, reindeer, elk, whitetail and mule deer, the moose is the world's largest deer and the largest of all antlered animals. One of seven subspecies, two in Asia, one in Europe and four in North America, the moose got its name from the Algonquin Indians who called it "mong-soa" meaning "twig-eater," which the early European settlers phonetically understood to be "moose."

Less social than most antlered animals, moose for the most part are solitary. They never move in herds, and even groups of moose are not often seen. If moose are seen together, it is probably because of a good feeding opportunity in the area; or they are a group of younger bulls, or yearlings, staying away from the old bulls during the rutting, or breeding, season; or it is a bull moose with a small harem of cows during the rutting season.

Traveling mostly independently of one another, these unusual animals have no leaders or social pecking order. Dominance of one animal over another only comes into play during the rutting season when bulls fight each other over cows.

And fight they do, with their remarkable antlers, their most unique physical feature. That impressive crown of solid bone, found only on the males, can weigh an astounding 60 to 85 pounds when full grown, often with a 6-foot spread. (The record belongs to an Alaskan moose with a spread of 77½ inches.)

Antler growth begins in early April, but the slight bulges aren't really noticeable until the month's end. Then the twin swellings become "velvet" knobs. The so-called velvet is soft skin minutely covered with fine hair masking the small flexible bony structure. It contains tiny blood vessels that nourish the developing antlers and stimulate their growth.

Technically known as "pedicels" (small stalks), the two projections of the frontal bone push up into swellings midway between the eyes and ears and eventually grow out nearly at right angles to the head before making their dramatic spreading sweep upward. During this period moose are very careful of the "growing stalks." If this early stage pedicel is damaged, the deformity to the antler that occurs will be permanent, even though new antlers grow every year.

During May and June, the new antlers grow swiftly and by the middle of July the bony structure is about two-thirds complete. By the middle of August, the antlers are fully grown, and the hardening, or ossification, process begins at the base, then progresses upward until the entire spongy antler spread becomes steel hard.

Now, that velvet skin containing the blood vessels begins to dry and peel off. The moose helps it along by rubbing his antlers against bushes and trees. When all the cushioning, nourishing velvet has vanished, the phenomenon that began just four months ago is complete. The antlers are sharp, white and hard, but as the moose continues to rub them against trees and bushes, the color soon turns to tan, then brown. Only the points remain white, smooth, shiny and saber sharp.

The moose's antlers are the key to all moose survival. No two sets are alike. They range from twisted, swordlike blades, to broad, dished or flat palmate shapes (like the large open palm of a hand). The antlers do not reach their magnificent full size until the moose's sixth year. Young bulls grow their first set, which is only 6 to 10 inches long, at sixteen months. The following year the antlers grow longer and have prongs on both sides. At forty months the antlers begin to take on the typical impressive flattened appearance. At four years, the antlers are the normal adult form, palmate but still small.

How do these great beasts with their cumbersome, protruding antlers manage to make their way through the thick forests and tall tangles of brush without getting hung up? Naturalists believe that moose have excellent depth perception and are accurate judges of the negotiability of areas. They also have been observed turning their heads sideways when moving through narrow spaces.

Along with the development of that remarkable rack of horns, comes the reproductive, or mating, urge that reaches its peak in September, beginning a two month rutting period. Whatever the age of the bull, the first stage of the rutting urge begins with the shedding, or tattering, of antler velvet, with bulls practicing for contests to come by butting trees, or engaging in pushing matches with other bulls the same age. Carefully placing their antlers together, a pair of bulls shove each other around.

Males younger than four years don't stand much of a chance with older, stronger bulls with larger antlers and when challenged turn and trot away. Only at this time will these younger bulls, or yearlings, gather together, feeding, moving, resting, and sometimes mock-fighting by hooking their small antlers at one another.

But contests are serious business for mature bulls. Witnesses call fights between them one of the most awesome combats in nature.

"I watched a struggle between big bulls for twenty minutes," reported E. B. Bailey of Quebec's Department of Fish and Game. "The bulls knocked down trees 3 and 4 inches in diameter as they battled. When it was ended, it looked as if a bulldozer had worked over about an acre of ground."

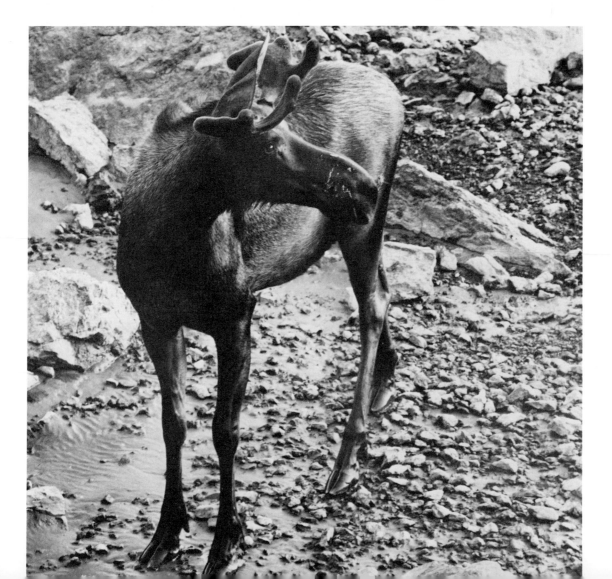

On a journey of less than 500 miles in Alaska, biologist Frank Dufresne found fourteen bulls killed in battle, three pairs with their antlers locked in death.

During the rutting season, the bull's neck becomes swollen, his eyes bloodshot, his temper short, he becomes a fearsome, belligerent beast with a one-track mind. He travels widely, eating little, searching for willing females and fighting bulls that contest his choice of a mate.

A battle is about to begin when bulls approach each other walking stiff-legged, with lowered muzzles, ears laid back, manes bristling. Then they rush forward and meet head to head, antlers rattling against antlers. Once locked together each animal tries to push the other off balance. If one bull slips, stumbles or is pushed off balance, the other instantly strikes hard with lowered antlers, hitting at the chest, ribs and legs. Sometimes this is enough to discourage the opponent, and he will wheel around and leave the battlefield.

If, however, the contest seems to be a stalemate, the menacing bulls will stay near each other for a week or more, until one finally gives up and leaves for less challenging territory. Often during these contests the cow stands placidly by, seeming to ignore the whole affair.

A bull and a cow first get together through a series of mating calls, among the few calls moose make. Moose will bark in alarm somewhat like a deer; calves whine to attract their mothers or bleat in distress, and the mother will grunt sharply to summon her calf; but for the most part moose are rather silent creatures.

If the bull initiates the call, he moos loudly in clear, sirenlike tones, and the cow responds, alternating shrill moos with coarse bawlings. If the cow is the first to call, she wails loudly and clearly. The male then responds to her call with a series of deep, carrying, drumlike grunts. He also grunts to signal his readiness to mate with any nearby cow.

Often the cow may hear the bull's invitation to mate while standing thigh-deep in the waters of a lake or pond. She will call in response and quickly leave the water to find the male where he stands in brush or under trees on the shore, guiding her to him with his piercing bellows.

In an unusual courtship tactic, the bull moose will sometimes find soft ground and, using both forefeet and antlers, dig out a wallow deep enough to hold both himself and any cow that may be enticed. Once the wallow is finished, the male stretches out in it and waits. Quite often cows in estrus, ready to be bred, and attracted by the male's scent, will climb into the wallow and lie beside the bull.

Some bulls use a wallow to attract a number of cows, then forming a harem of ten or more. Whether the bull mates with all the cows hasn't been determined, and harems aren't common in most areas. The practice seems most prevalent in Alaska's Mount McKinley National Park area where harems have often been seen.

During the rutting period older cows will drive away the younger females so that interested males won't be distracted. Adult cows sometimes fight over the attention of a bull, using their sharp hooves.

A bull and a cow may stay together for about ten days, then the bull will leave her to seek out and mate with several other cows before his fire and strength are gone.

Gaunt now from lack of food and his strenuous activities, the bull docilely joins a small group of equally placid bulls and cows. With the rutting season over and winter approaching, his antlers become a useless weight and are discarded in late December by knocking them forcibly against trees, to grow again the following spring. The cycle benefits the bull during the difficult winter months when survival would be much more difficult if he were still carrying that heavy crown of bone.

About eight months after the bull and cow have mated, usually in June, the female gives birth to a 25- to 30-pound calf. Twins are rare, appearing only about 15 percent of the time, and triplets are even rarer. For the birth the cow seeks an isolated place, on an island if available, where any other animal's approach is easily detected by sound as it swims, or deep in a swamp or heavy thicket. The cow carefully conceals her offspring for three days, or until it is strong enough to follow her about. But timing is dependent upon the circumstances. One calf, no more than three hours old, followed its alarmed mother as rapidly as it could move for 500 yards over rough terrain that included a steep hill.

Born with its eyes open, the newborn calf stands about 30 inches at the shoulder and is 40 inches long. Its coat is reddish brown, its head paler, with dark rings around the eyes and a dark muzzle.

The calf begins to nurse about one hour after birth, with the tall cow squatting so the calf can reach her teats. The calf feeds for one to two minutes at a time. After most feedings the calf rests in a hidden place, the cow close by.

In three or four days the calf easily follows its mother who moves slowly, carefully avoiding obstacles and terrain where the calf would have difficulty maneuvering. The female is extremely protective, ready to strike anything if it approaches her offspring too closely, be it human, animal or machine. She warns intruders off by rearing up like an angry stallion and striking the air with her forefeet. In Alaska, one cow repeatedly tried to strike a helicopter that was hovering closely, trying to photograph her and her calf.

Few creatures of any kind will challenge a huge, protective, unpredictable female moose with calf. Exception: dedicated photographers. In Alaska, the photographer who made this book possible was charged by a moose with calf and violently hurled to the ground. Luckily, the cow just knocked him over and did not use her knife-sharp hooves.

At ten days of age the moose calf can outrun a person. But despite this ability, calf mortality is greatest during those first two weeks. Poor physical condition at birth, cold, wet weather, drowning, predators, especially bears and wolves, are factors that weigh against the life expectancy of the little moose.

Both wolves and bears will try to separate the mother from the helpless calf, wolves sometimes working in teams or packs. Buffalo, and some other animals that travel in herds, use the strength of many to defeat or discourage persistent predators. The solitary moose is more vulnerable.

However, if moose calves make it to a month old they have an excellent chance of outrunning a bear. Wolves are something else, especially in winter when the snow is no more than 2 feet deep and doesn't hamper the wolf's speed and pack tactics. Deeper snow aids the long-legged moose. Although wolves will readily take unprotected calves, they often prey on weak, ill and old adults, which is actually beneficial to the moose as a species.

Under normal conditions the main activity of the well-protected and well-fed calf seems to be growing—fast. For the first month it gains 2 pounds every day, and 4 pounds daily after that.

It is difficult for natural scientists to deduce the exact milk intake of a wild calf, but it was recorded that a two-week-old calf in captivity drank a quart of evaporated milk half-diluted with water three times each day. At nine weeks the amount was increased to 2 gallons a day. Experts believe that wild calves may consume somewhat less at each feeding but will nurse more often. With adequate feeding, by the end of August the calf's weight has grown to 150 to 200 pounds.

Some natural scientists believe that no animal in North America grows so rapidly as the moose. Naturalist Joe Van Wormer reports that the growth record of captive calves showed a gain of from 115 to 215 pounds in three and one half months. The calves' weight reached 400 to 600 pounds in the first year; a two-year-old bull's weight jumped to 700 pounds, a three-year-old's to 900 pounds.

By the end of the second month, the calf begins to imitate the mother and starts browsing on tender leaves. This, with the addition of milk from somewhat reduced nursing, still adds 5 pounds to its weight daily.

By mid-August the calf is officially weaned, even though it will nurse much longer if the mother will permit it. Half-grown bulls nearly the size of their mothers have been observed still trying to nurse.

As summer ends, the calf's appearance changes. Its reddish brown coat is now a very dark, grayish brown, shoulders and neck silver gray, the face brown, the legs lighter brown. The calf is now a small replica of its mother.

Winter finds the cow with triple responsibilities. She must feed and care for herself, for her six-month-old calf would not survive through the winter without her. And, if she is pregnant, which is probable, the health of the calf she carries depends upon her condition and how well she eats and physically survives the harsh winter months when food isn't plentiful.

Through the ages that have destroyed lesser species, moose have been superb survivors, so the odds are good that the normal pattern of life will persist. In early June the cow will have her healthy new calf, and last year's yearling, be it female or bull, will be driven away to continue its own mostly solitary life cycle.

It will be well prepared. The female moose has a strong maternal instinct and does much for her offspring besides protecting and feeding it. She has taught it the arts of backtracking, circling and coming up behind its enemy, of standing motionless in thickets, taking advantage of natural camouflage, of moving silently and swiftly when danger is scented from afar and avoiding it before it arrives.

Although that well-mothered moose calf will grow into the largest antlered animal on earth, despite its size its coloring will protect it and almost paint it out of its surroundings. In tall brush or tree second growth the brownish black back and sides and the yellowish white legs blend into the foliage. And the moose knows it, almost from birth.

This camouflage is effective against humans, the moose's number one enemy, but something special is needed for protection against keener-eyed predators.

Besides its inborn instincts and parental training, the young moose comes physically well equipped to face the dangers ahead. Although its eyesight is not especially good, its senses of smell and hearing are impressive weapons of defense. One moose calf scented a man a mile away, enabling it to quickly hide in a thicket. In one experiment, a biologist found that the moose's hearing may be unequaled: Two moose were keenly aware of the footsteps of a man, softly, carefully approaching, fully two minutes before the scientist could detect the sound of the footsteps that he was prepared for and waiting to hear.

The moose's hooves provide another defense: With tremendous power behind them, the hooves can break the back or crush the skull of almost any adversary. E. B. Bailey of Quebec's Department of Fish and Game saw a young bull moose kill an adult black bear by pounding its head and back with his front hooves. Moose also have been seen killing a wolf with one blow of a front hoof, or a kick from a hind foot.

But the grizzly is a more serious enemy than wolves or black bears. Although adult moose, except where their calves are concerned, do not seem to regard the black bear with overt fear or caution, they avoid grizzlies whenever possible. For not only are they a serious threat to the calves, but adult grizzlies can and do prey upon adult moose. Unless the moose is in its prime and healthy, it doesn't stand much of a chance against the big yellowish brown bear. With its cunning, weight, claws, fangs and hunting and killing skill, a grizzly has been observed besting an adult moose, dragging it down and killing it, despite its sharp and skillful hooves. But even in perfect fighting trim, a moose would rather run than fight. And it can outrun a grizzly.

The moose's hooves, often 7 inches long, aided by large dewclaws, provide more than defense. The dewclaws, horny projections on the back of each leg above the hoof, give the animal additional purchase power in bogs, mud and snow. The hooves, more flexible, with a greater division than those of most hoofed animals, enable the moose to spread his "toes" to improve his footing. Consequently, moose can walk in areas that other large creatures, including humans, would find impassible. Naturalists have been amazed to see a 1,000-pound animal cross a swamp where a person would have difficulty walking. The speed and grace with which a moose negotiates mossy, slippery, rocky terrain and hurdles the hazard of tangled fallen trees is unbelievable. They can move their great bulk silently even through heavy cover, and they also appear to be experts at knowing when ice will support them.

As ungainly and short-legged as the moose looks, it has another asset that would appear to be highly unlikely, speed. It is agreed that a moose can outrun a horse, especially on home territory, and in a race the wolf can't compete. One moose was clocked at 35 miles an hour for a distance of a quarter of a mile. Another ran steadily for a mile at about 20 miles an hour. In a normal trot one cow traveled a mile over rough terrain in less than ten minutes.

The creature's stamina also is impressive. A harness-broken moose drew a sleigh 160 miles on the frozen Saint John River in New Brunswick, Canada, showing no signs of fatigue. These creatures that emerged from the brutal cold of the Ice Age have been observed at Grand Teton National Park at an elevation of 9,000 feet in the dead of winter, graphically proving their ruggedness by moving through 6 feet of snow. Sometimes in that deep powder, if its long legs can't get it through, the moose kneels and uses its chest to plow the snow, its back legs providing the forward pushing power.

Moose are well-armed for survival in the cold. Their 4-inch body hair although brittle is thick and filled with air cells that help to conserve body heat. In the winter moose "yard," several moose trampling the snow down to give them a space to move around in, also trampling pathways for easier traveling when they search for food. Using those versatile hoofs they chop through ice and paw through snow to find plant life. They also straddle young trees, forcing them down within reach, and eat the choice slender branches and twigs.

But winter is hard even for these remarkable creatures. Besides predators and the weather, unremitting and impossible to defeat, winter brings another enemy, moose, or winter, ticks. These biting, blood-sucking insects appear late in the season making life difficult. Without the relief of ponds and lakes in which to immerse themselves to discourage the pests, moose resort to scratching the insects off with their hind feet, rubbing against trees and shrubs. As many as 500 ticks have been found on each ear of a moose. If an animal is run-down from malnutrition the insects can cause its death. But only the weak are brought down by the persistent ticks. Most moose survive as they have for much more than a millennium.

When spring arrives moose bring another major talent into play. They are among the most skillful swimmers in the mammal world. Soon after birth, the calf is led into shallow water by its mother, then the next day into deeper water until finally the calf is forced to swim as it follows its parent. In a matter of days the young moose has mastered the lesson.

Cows with young calves have been observed swimming a half mile or more across a lake. Sometimes a calf rests head or forefeet on the mother's haunches, but usually the young swim independently, often bleating as they swim. Sometimes the female swims back to check on the calf's progress, then proceeds at a somewhat slower pace, grunting, seeming to encourage her offspring to keep up the good work.

An unweaned calf will often be seen swimming out to where the mother is feeding in a lake or pond. It will swim around her, nudging her, trying to get her to return to shore so it can nurse. Failing, the calf swims back to shore. Sometimes the calf just swims out to its mother as an exercise, then returns to shore and rests until the female finishes feeding.

Two canoeists on a lake deep in the Canadian wilderness were astounded to see a bull moose suddenly rise to the surface from where it had been feeding on the bottom. It popped up abruptly, cascading water, pondweeds hanging from its mouth, looking like a mythical sea monster with its big mule's nose, 5-foot spread of shovel-flat antlers and slick brown black hide.

Teams of canoe experts have also been surprised to learn that although they could keep up with a steadily swimming moose they could not pass it. Powerful, assured swimmers, moose can swim a steady 6 miles an hour and have been clocked swimming for 12 miles without stopping. They also are determined swimmers and will not stop for anything less than a large boat.

In an Alaskan lake one naturalist saw a moose with a very young calf outswim a large grizzly bear with two half-grown cubs. The moose and calf reached shore with plenty of time to easily outdistance the hungry bears on land.

Although moose will swim and even lie in water to escape summer flies and mosquitoes, or roll in mud to protectively coat themselves, they swim for two basic reasons: to travel the shortest distance between two points, and to feed.

They feed on underwater plants and on floating plants even while swimming. The aquatic plants that they like are eelgrass, pond lilies, pondweeds, water shield, wild celery and wild rice, but they eat a wide variety of other plants and also have been observed avidly feeding on algae.

Feeding for an hour at a time, they dive and fill their mouths with underwater plants, then, depending upon water depth, either surface or lift their heads out of the water to swallow the food. They are known to dive in water 20 feet deep to feed on bottom growth. While being timed, some moose fed underwater every five seconds. It is common for them to remain underwater for one full minute. In his study of moose on Michigan's Isle Royale, naturalist Adolph Murie saw a moose dive to the bottom of a lake and remain submerged for a minute and a half.

When feeding in shallow water, moose submerge their heads just up to the ears, which move about above the surface, radarlike, as the animal listens for danger sounds.

Water plants are eaten mainly in early summer when they are tender. As the season passes the plants become tough and unpalatable. Moose feed on water plants more often in eastern North America than they do in states like Montana and Wyoming. A study there came up with surprising information. Although "browsers," eaters of leaves and twigs of trees and woody plants, this study showed that except in winter when browsing is the main feeding activity, moose eat over 70 percent forbs (plants and herbs not considered grass), more than 20 percent browse, the remainder grass.

On a normal day, a moose starts moving just before dawn, feeds until the middle of the morning, then rests. When it beds down (for four or five hours before feeding again in late evening) it finds a place where it is concealed, but located so it can make a fast exit if necessary. It is the natural magic of the moose that a 1,000-pound animal can literally vanish in a small growth of willows.

Willow is the moose's favorite food, but it likes leaves, twigs and slender branches of most trees, and also enjoys the bark from trees in the spring, when the sap is almost ready to run. It uses its large teeth as scrapers to shred the bark off the tree trunks. It nips off twigs by taking the twig between its lower incisors and the premaxillaries of its upper jaw, having no upper incissors, and jerking its head upward. Leaves are stripped from a branch by pulling it sideways through the mouth.

About half the browsing is at heights of 2 to 4 feet above the ground, but if necessary the moose can reach to 10 feet by standing on its hind legs. It prefers open places for foraging, with water close by, and does best in areas with second-growth shrubs and saplings. Although considered forest animals, moose do poorly in areas where trees are full grown.

Moose remain where food is abundant, and may feed in a growth of young willows for two weeks. They progress slowly while feeding, covering only a few yards at a time. Feeding is steady; one big bull was observed eating for almost two hours without a break. One of the favorite sights of moose-watchers occurs in the spring when the animals, eager for young green grass, kneel and graze for hours without standing up.

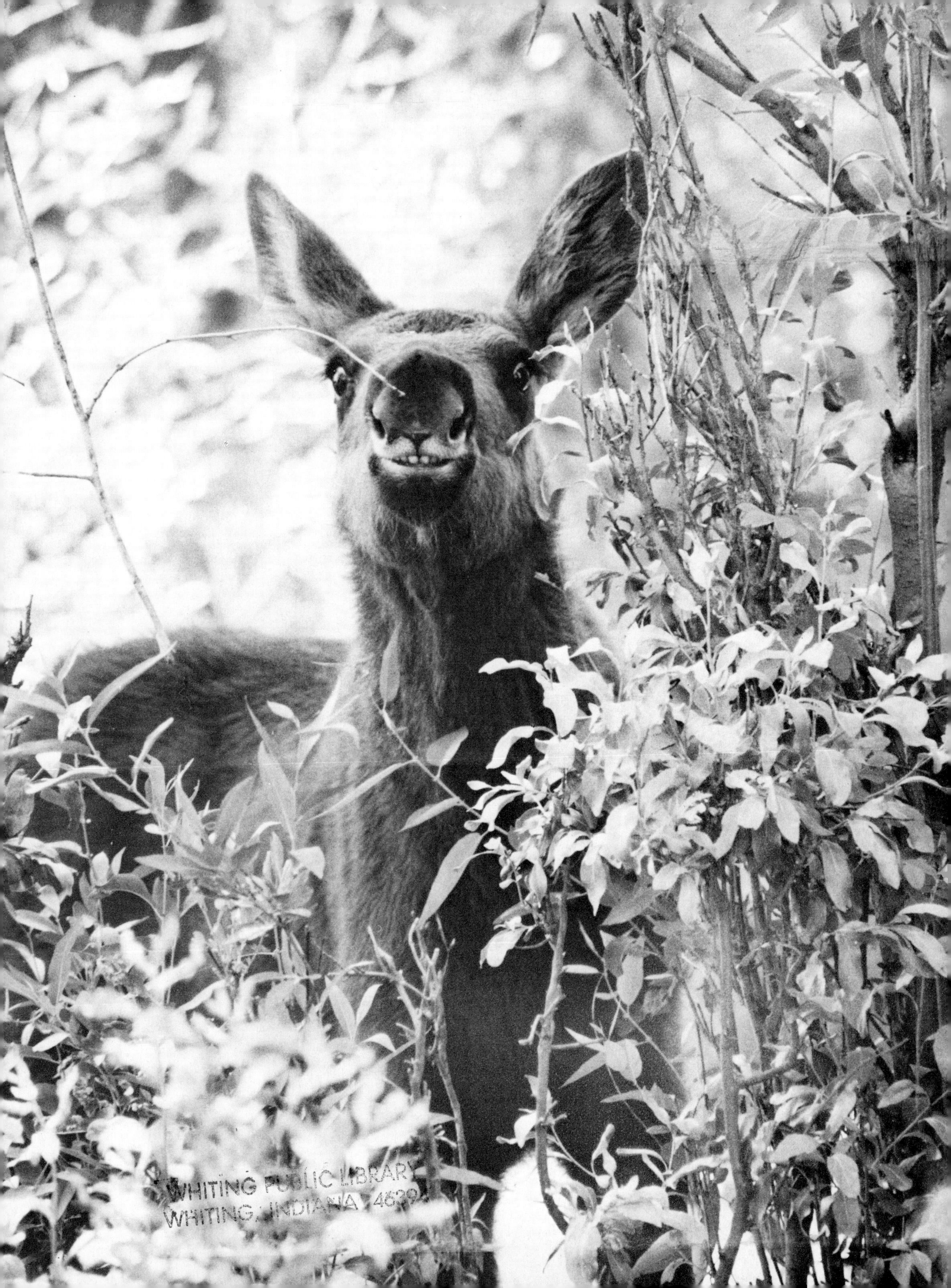

They are big eaters, needing 40 to 50 pounds of food a day in winter and 50 to 60 in summer, which comprises a monthly consumption of between 1,200 and 1,500 pounds of feed, more than the weight of the average moose.

Moose are ruminants—cud chewers. That seemingly constant chewing is an important part of their digestive process. They take in food quickly, chewing leaves, twigs, plants just enough so the mass can be swallowed. The swallowed food goes into the rumen, or first section of a four-compartment stomach. There bacteria prepares it for digestion. Bacterial action continues as the food passes into the reticulum, the second stomach section. The pulp that remains, the cud, is returned to the mouth, where it is amply rechewed, then again swallowed and passed into the third, then the fourth stomach compartment where it is absorbed.

Cud-chewing adult moose have been timed at 82 contented "chews" a minute, some calves at 120.

After eating and resting, moose are fond of stretching. Looking like a great cat arising after a nap, a moose extends its head and neck full length, its nose pointing almost straight up; next the legs are stretched straight out to the sides one at a time, then straight forward.

An oddity: Moose will sometimes join a herd of grazing horses to feed, but never will mingle with cattle.

The moose's life span is believed to be 20 years, but averages ten. It is not uncommon for moose to spend their entire lives within 10 or 15 miles of where they were born. This depends, of course, on food supply. Their total range area usually does not encompass more than 1½ square miles—which almost brought about their downfall.

Indians believed the moose to be an omen of good, and they also thought that by eating its meat they would gain its strength. In the frontier days, it was thought that the left hind foot of the moose was a certain cure for epilepsy, that bone rings made from the antlers banished headache and dizziness, and that mixed with various herbs, ground antler was an antidote for snakebite. The hooves were believed to cure more than 600 diseases or afflictions.

So-called sportsmen, Indians and market hunters killed moose of any age or sex during any season, until in Maine, parts of Canada and the West this great animal so dwindled in numbers by the mid-forties that it was thought that soon it would have the same fate as the buffalo.

But conservationists and other far-sighted people finally prevailed. The leader among them, Dr. Henry Fairfield Osborn, then president of the New York Zoological Society, said, "Nature has been millions of years in developing that wonderful animal, and man should not ruthlessly destroy him."

To our credit we haven't. Today, most states have either abolished hunting of moose or have short, stringently controlled seasons.

Gordon C. Haber has summed up the success story of the moose in the language of the naturalist: "The moose," he wrote, "ranks as one of the most biologically successful of the large northern mammals. Having colonized a wide diversity of habitats across both hemispheres, it has persisted over most of these regions despite sustained exploitation by humans, wolves and bears."

Having survived another age perhaps even more dangerous than the Ice Age, the moose now appears to be here to stay.